SHANNON WEBB-CAMPBELL is an award-winning poet, writer, and journalist of mixed Aboriginal ancestry. She is the inaugural winner of Egale Canada's *Out in Print Award* and was the Canadian Women in Literary Arts 2014 critic-in-residence. *Still No Word* is her first collection of poems. She lives in Halifax.

ACKNOWLEDGEMENTS

Some of these poems first appeared in *Riddle Fence*, *The Coast*, and *Plenitude Magazine*. Thanks to the editors.

"Harvest Your Heart" was made into a video poem by Krista Davis, and exhibited at Creative Nova Scotia Awards 2014.

Lyrics from "Kepmite'tmnej (Honour Song)," performed by Sentanneway Kengnamogwom Native Choir, Conne River, Newfoundland, are used in the poem "Kepmite'tmnej (Honour Song)."

Lyrics from "Smoke Gets in Your Eyes," by The Platters, are used in the poem "Last View of Bell Island."

Maltese proverbs are used in the poem "Mal'ta Venus."

Gratitude to the Mi'kmaw territory and people, who witness dawn first, and acknowledgement that I live (and write) on unceded Indigenous land.

Thank you to our ancestors who made it possible we're still here, and to honour the generations who will come after us.

A heartfelt thanks to the formidable tribes at Breakwater Books, editor James Langer in particular, Egale Canada Human Rights Trust, my teachers and comrades at the University of British Columbia, especially Susan Musgrave, Qalipu Mi'kmaq First Nation, Zab Design & Typography, and Canadian Women in Literary Arts for their generous support and recognition.

Thank you to my parents, the ever-extending branches of my family tree, all of my wild-hearted friends near and far, the Atlantic Ocean, and a knowing wink to you.

Shannon Webb-Campbell

Still No Word

BREAKWATER

P.O. BOX 2188, ST. JOHN'S, NL, CANADA, A1C 6E6
WWW.BREAKWATERBOOKS.COM

LIBRARY AND ARCHIVES CANADA CATALOGUING IN PUBLICATION
Webb-Campbell, Shannon, 1983-, author
Still no word / Shannon Webb-Campbell.
Poems.
ISBN 978-1-55081-588-7 (pbk.)
I. Title.

PS8645.E225S75 2015 C811'.6 C2014-908405-6

DESIGN Zab Design & Typography

TYPEFACE *Cardea* by David Cabianca (Emigre)

We acknowledge the support of the Canada Council for the Arts, which last year invested $157 million to bring the arts to Canadians throughout the country. We acknowledge the financial support of the Government of Canada through the Canada Book Fund (CBF) and the Government of Newfoundland and Labrador through the Department of Tourism, Culture and Recreation for our publishing activities.

Canada Council for the Arts | Conseil des Arts du Canada

Newfoundland Labrador

Breakwater Books is committed to choosing papers and materials for our books that help to protect our environment. To this end, this book is printed on a recycled paper that is certified by the Forest Stewardship Council®.

For my grandmother, Amelia Beattie
(1935–2013), we'll always be as thick as thieves,
and for my great-great grandmother,
Mary Webb (1881–1978)

Contents

Still No Word

Harvest Your Heart

When you arrive at this loneliness write a letter to each lover and examine what was taken. Remind them with memories and pinpoint subtle ways they touched you. Recall the way they buttered your toast and spread your thighs.

Bring them to your tower, where you've been hiding since you left them, learning and unlearning, doing and undoing, covering and recovering. Cup your hands over their eyes and linger until anxiety turns to ease, familiarity.

You know the years have worn on them; they've worn on you, too.

Give them a moment to adjust, to take in the view. Ask them to bear witness to your shame, a transformation of pain, reclaimed.

Tell them of the centuries you've spent grieving. Give them, and yourself, mercy. Apologize before a harvest moon. Set right what can be set right and finally drop what you couldn't let go of. Hold your own hand, and kiss your palms goodnight.

Love again, this stranger in you. Set a table for two and forget to blow out the candles before bed. Burn down the house and build anew.

What's My Soul Name? Ask Me Again and I'll Tell You the Same

My name is not legal. It's stolen, an homage to Vikings, who travelled from that shore to this. There is no certificate to prove I was born, only a blank page: no date, birthplace, or given name.

For two weeks my name was an asterisk. Without a sense of itself, my name became a symbol, something that indicated separateness and aggregate. My name cannot read nor write.

My name couldn't recognize itself if called. It once swam from the Galapagos Islands to San Francisco without stopping. No sharks or mermaids approached it. My name doesn't speak a language.

My name doesn't pay taxes, bills, or wash dishes. It was mute and taken in by a hydrologist, who didn't believe in towel drying, and a llama farmer, who taught my name how to spin and felt cloth.

My name questioned the philosophical underpinnings of eternal recurrence. Thus I was born, but not.

The universe has imposed years of heaviness on my name. I have demanded it right itself, to meet its maker. I have tried to help it discover itself. To take it out for cocktails and meet new people.

My name doesn't know how to hold its alcohol, or the weight of its shame.

Emotional Philosophy

How the light is sad.
How it will not leave us alone.
How we are tugged up staircases
by the way it angles across landings.
Or just our faces — tipped
to the clear, depleted sky.
— JAN ZWICKY, "April"

I haven't wondered why you painted the house
primary colours.
I've noticed the red staircase, yellow banister, purple
kitchen.

I haven't noted each room feels like a page in a
children's book.
I've learned you picked bright hues to keep the blues
at bay.

I haven't counted 248 green tiles in the kitchen.
I've made meals I didn't eat only to pass an hour.

I haven't wondered if we'd get along.
I've imagined you boiling the kettle.

I haven't refilled the saltshaker on the stove.
I've stopped taking sugar in my tea.

I haven't cleaned out the chicken in the freezer.
I've taken out the compost.

I haven't finished all the expensive whisky.
I've mixed pink ladies with your gin.

I haven't fingered the bookshelves in the living room.
I've read *The Bell Jar* you bought for a dollar a year
before I was born.

I haven't watered your dead plants, certain they'll come
back to life.
I've curled under wool blankets, and into your pillows.

I haven't looked through your photo albums.
I've memorized that dress you wore on New Year's Eve,
1997.

I haven't danced myself to *Rumours* on repeat.
I've memorized the lyrics to "Gypsy."

I haven't opened the windows to let the house breathe.
I've closed the blinds to keep strangers from looking in.

I haven't folded my thoughts into your dusty drawers.
I've watched the shadows fall over each room.

I haven't listened to your housekeeper sing Portuguese
lullabies.
I've paid her fifty dollars every other week.

I haven't rearranged the furniture.

I've arranged fresh cut wildflowers from your garden.

I haven't kept the flowers in the bathtub away from the
orange tabby.
I've wondered what makes a cat meow.

I haven't used up all your ballpoint pens.
I've borrowed some pages from an old notebook.

I haven't opened your unpaid bills.
I've read your old magazines and put your death
certificate aside.

I haven't discovered the manuscript in your office.
I've made a photocopy.

I haven't slept soundly every night.
I've been napping above the covers.

I haven't heard the crows in the trees in morning.
I've wondered what side of the bed was yours.

I haven't longed to dream beside someone.
I've cried myself to sleep on your knobby sheets.

I haven't finished the shampoo left on the edge of the tub.
I've used the last Q-tip.

I haven't found watches all over the place.
I've wondered the purpose of time if it's wrong.

I haven't paid off all my library fines.
I've taken out armfuls of books to have something to
return.

I haven't weeded.
I've swept the leaves from the step.

I haven't taken up smoking.
I've put cigarettes out behind the shed.

I haven't ordered take out every other night.
I've found greens in the vegetable garden.

I haven't worried about your lover.
I've brought her blue towel to the beach.

I haven't calculated 4974 miles between Maynard
Street and Edmonton.
I've wondered what drew you to Alaska.

I haven't wondered what causes cancer.
I've questioned the philosophy of emotions.

I haven't avoided the bottles of orange pills.
I've read the pages you wrote in your last days.

I haven't understood the abbreviated medication
dosages.
I've found the poems written between hours of
methadone and Xanax.

I haven't seen a doctor.
I've read *Songs for Relinquishing the Earth.*

I haven't thought she's watching over me like you
noted in the margins.
I've believed you were.

Towards Definition

Poetry is language. Poetry is suspicion. Poetry is what it isn't.
Poetry is sneaky. Poetry is groundwork and subtext.
Poetry is visceral,
is relic.

Poetry is silence, curiosity, hurricane, regrowth.
Poetry is bleach, intimacy,
pillow creases,
and quiet.

Poetry is belly up to the bar, is ocean, inversion, weather, is
masturbation, guesswork, high tide. Poetry

is low tide. Poetry is gospel, is vacant, is Perseids
and undergrowth.

Poetry is cartography:
mapmakers and sailors
trust it's
written in the stars.

Big Muise Island

a tree leans over a lake on Big Muise
strives for another shoreline
reaches for more
the appeal: always wanting to
be away from where we are
an attempt to uproot, escape a past,
to get off the island
branches only make the water's edge
halfway between grass and lake,
a stump grows, almost like a leg,
stretches to steel itself
an anchor for the large-toothed aspen
to hold on to

as roots grow restless

Point Mistaken

I mistook you for someone else
walking over ancient rocks
your feet covered in blue socks
to preserve the fossils

I saw something new in you

your brown eyes softened
as your calloused fingers traced
the remnants
of all that came before us

time began
under your fingernails

on the drive home
a whale breached
and we pulled over
struck by seeing something
larger than ourselves

Journey Lullaby (Inside the Gramophone)

The light gives of itself
to anyone who knows to receive it
without demanding it to eliminate
the night.
— Author unknown

there are days when I need you
there are days when you're just there

on this lonesome journey
all these unknown prayers

it took so long for me to need you
it took so long for you to dare

no more hard worn feelings
no more sad pressed cares

love is long
and unyielding

love is long
and unfair

on this lonesome journey
all these unknown prayers

Cape Race

Can you hear the distress call of my affection?

it's a bloated foghorn, a muted trumpet,
a whale's cry, a seabird stranded mid-migration

put your hand on my chest,
listen to its squall, feel the heat of my salt-stained skin

the ocean reminds us, we're alive,
we're above air, and below water

we retreated into each other
until the lighthouse cracked

our closed minds open,
our silent hearts roar

Cod-Jigger and the Shark

before she became a broken-necked woman in a hospital bed,
sores on her legs, cysts that exploded

before a 60 pound body,
the worst gallstones

before her organs dropped from the orchard of her skeleton,
bottomed out, rearranged their place,
bones passed the ability to heal

before hours measured by morphine and morphine,
she pulled off the oxygen mask,
couldn't take being alive

before her mother finally heard her,
when her pneumonia-soaked butterfly lungs collapsed,
and she could finally let go

before she found God, and screamed for 12 hours straight,
her mouth like a child: Mommy, Daddy, take me now

when she returned to the earth's crust,
all wisdom and ocean, out cod-jigging,
and the only one to catch a porbeagle shark

The Fog Seeker

an island of dreamers
where seaweed hangs
damp, limp in the trees
and a man spent 60 years of his life
collecting jars of fog
finding life's temperament
on an unknown island
in the midst of a mighty bay

a world renowned
atmospheric scientist,
a cloud physicist
with a lifetime of jam jars
fog-filled detailing the buildup
and decline of acidity
from pollution in fog banks
to levels of mercury

an internal investigation on what it means
to follow wonder, explore it,
and establish relationships to mystery
or the way water cycles balance

even as a boy he checked the forecast twice a day,
kept record of events in a notebook
could tell a weather report from
traces of sky, weight of air
or pressure in atmosphere

he created a device to measure
vapour pressure changes,
the structure of clouds catalogued by shape,

type, height, and density,
screened for elemental personalities

ice: his first word as a child
now an old man, losing language, living on Grand Manan,
with thousands of mason jars of clear water
under the stairs scattered in rows

not necessarily in line
a body of work on acid rain

A Sixty-Tonne Blue Whale Slowly Rots

town clerk smells 26 meters of beached whale, tries
to find a way to get rid of it before it explodes

scientists tell her to stay away from the carcass, it
carries viruses, bacteria

the town draws different visitors

concerns of methane gas, decomposition

clerk cries—we don't have any resources, we don't
have expertise!

clocks tick on solutions, a swollen whale grows

as the weather warmed, things only got worse

The Octogenarian

you were born under
an orphan moon,
once a son,
three times a father,
a grandfather,
now widower

you were an electrician,
a foreman in Churchill Falls,
a daily newspaper reader,
the best eater around

now, you are becoming
something new —
an octogenarian
not an octopus
or vegetarian

you've earned your keep,
paid your dues,
own many pairs of big shoes

today you can sit back,
take in the view,
the dawn of a new era
feet up,
two breakfasts,
long naps,
one finger of scotch,
always leave
room for dessert

Needs vs Wants

I need water.   I want salt.
    I need oxygen.   I want air.
I need touch.   I want sex.

I need food.   I want nourishment.
          I need company.   I want love.
               I need security.   I want trust.
I need shelter. I want sanctuary.
       I need art.   I want expression.
    I need family.   I want community.

I need affection. I want desire.

      I need nature.   I want ocean.

    I need to wander.   I want to be still.

               I need intrigue.   I want stability.

I need a lover.   I want a partner.
    I need to read.   I want to be read.

Modern Astronomy

had I known your constellation of lovers
I would have understood

your need to return to the pines

had I known you drank
to get close to the words

had I known you looked to the sky

for stability and conflict

had I known you were only
in the state of being human

I would have understood
your inability to forgive

The Anthropology of Headache Weather

A found poem, combining fragments of an Anthropologie catalogue and "Headache Weather," by Evelyn Lau

This morning you wanted the world –
a thousand lights
like a paper lotus lantern
armfuls of frayed lilies, a whole Black Forest cake –
afloat, we set off,
reaching for a slow burning
passion for spring

It was headache weather –
add abstract strokes of colour
you gulped your pills: waited
ports of call
along the way
until we lay ourselves
down for a traveller's rest

It's almost a loss
the migraine you knew –
from our birds eye view

No handyman, you still spoke
we first imagine
a larger-than-life rising
structure along the glittering
waters,

its grip and grind at your temples
calling to mind
terraced winged beauties

Now opiates rush your bloodstream
a fine romance,
rain mists out of the golden sky,
enchanted by florals,
wrapped up in lace

On the Sidewalk

for Raymond Taavel

I stood on the sidewalk
where you were beaten
an embroidered heart woven
into a chain-link fence
reminded me of yours
each yard of yarn
tied a tether to your presence
the setting sun
thickened Gottingen
cleansing the April night
for a moment
you were glowing
on the sidewalk
where you died

Mal'ta Venus

you went to bed with a man
after he rescued you from African refugees
who circled you at Valetta's bus shelter

Bil-lejl in-nisa kollha xorta
(at night all women are alike)

you went to bed with a landlord
who let you use his shower
when you ran out of hot water;
you danced in a Maltese
summer home with a man
who invited you to dry off
in the sun on his rooftop,
who gave you a set of keys,
drove you around Senglea

Mara sa dahket bix-xitan
(a woman has even cheated the devil)

you were found in the arms of a dealer
after you swam together by sand dunes
serpent tattoos snaked around ankles

Il-mara bhall-lumija taghsarha u tarmiha
(a woman is like a lemon; you squeeze her and throw her away)

a man your father's age
whose hands tore your nightdress
while you slept
who took you to Mdina
the silent city, left you in October
to become a spirit doll

Between Duckworth and Water Street

ink has dried up

the ocean turned inside out

anchors float to the surface

whales sob in their sleep

the moon fell out of the sky

hearts no longer beat

lovers have lost their nerve

A Healer's Lune

Seek wounded healer,

cry out to unseen ancestors:

still no word.

Oracle of Tarock

I've been obsessively reading
my horoscope on my phone.
I stay up until midnight
so I can read
tomorrow's reading today,
tap three tarot cards,
then wake up and wish
I could have a new reading.

If fate forgets you
hold the oracle card
right side up

invite a guest
for dinner
speak only to your subconscious

will a blue sky
tug at the clouds
make it rain

pray if you don't believe
ask for Buddha
demand your heart relax

excuse the small animal
of your being
expect loss

rush the season
fake trust
insist on reason

reassure yourself
you are better off alone
even if you are lonely

give your soul away
extract it from your body
complicate emptiness

I've Been Sleeping Lifetimes Deep on a Deflated Air Mattress

I dreamt of Morpheus
leader of Oneiroi
for 500 hours

He came to me
in form of another
and plucked feathers
from my shoulder blades

I've been sleeping lifetimes deep
on a deflated air mattress
glacier blue
too far gone to feel
a breath of wind
Mother paces
the waiting room
for 21 days
and 21 nights

I am dancing slow-release
milligrams of morphine
into the ether
when I trip into my
grandfather's room
and flop on the airbed
I don't wake
even to taste vomit

Liquid fills my lungs
while my grandfather snores
through sunrise
Downstairs my grandmother
passes out cold
forehead on the coffee table
cigarette in hand

My mother hears my death rattle
through the bathroom wall
and cries out in emergency
When the paramedics arrive
they scoop me up
like a teenage newborn
and carry me to the ambulance

I lose muscle mass
memory
mobility
breathing only
through an endotracheal tube
A bedside monitor tracks
my heart rate
my blood pressure
and measures
oxygen saturation

I dreamt of Morpheus
leader of Oneiroi
for 500 hours
He came to me
in form of another

and plucked feathers
from my shoulder blades

It was my very best death
and I don't remember

New Year's Resolutions for the Future

To make a point of working overtime, making space for
forgetfulness, and lingering in isolation. To move into
loneliness, and wrestle with it.
To stop reading for pleasure, and for education.

Trust in others, the weakness of their hearts, and honour
the unhealthy relationships abandoned. Hold a grudge, and
never let go.
Don't trust in the season, and the time won't come for
everything.

Be devoted to mundane tasks, lie diligently, forgo your spirit.
Remain closed off, there is nothing more.

Stop looking.
Never ask questions.

Kedgeemakogee

No living tissue grows more rapidly than deer antlers.
— WIKIPEDIA

camping under full buck moon
rising, the time of year
when male deer grow
new antlers, begin with velvet bumps
on foreheads

we could only hope for such renewal

Aphorisms (A Rule of Thirds)

To stand outside your self is to be open.

Every step a march in the inevitable parade.

A labyrinth has one path with many twists and turns.

Kepmite'tmnej (Honour Song)

on the coldest day of winter
at the clearing,
where Long Pond froze over

seashell in one hand,
a fist-full of cedar and sage
in the other,
you pierce the snow bank with
a seabird's feather

you light sage
smudge
under boot soles
over your pants
onto winter jacket
and across your chest
down one arm, then the other
and above your cap

Keptmite'tmnej ta'n teli-l'nuulti'kw
Nikma'jtut mawita'nej

then you smudge
cedar under my boots
up my leggings
across my womb
and breasts, linger
over my heart
we lock eyes until
smoke dissolves

Kepmite'tmnej ta'n wetapeksulti'kw
Nikma'jtut apoqnmatultinej

you sing Kepmite'tmnej,
a Mi'kmaw honour song,
clouds of hot breath
hover around winter-bare trees
the song drifts across the lake

Apoqnmatultinej ta'n Kisu'lkw
Tel-ika'luski'kw ula wskitqamu'k

we walk back to the car
close to the road, you point
at healing plants, dark greens
poke out of paper-white snow

Citta Vittoriosa by Candlelight

An ancient city lit

from within by tiny jitterbug flames

cobblestone steps of oscillation

Letters to Berlin

I've written love letters to Berlin. I've been soaked in
greed, sweat, and sin. I've played the pious and siren.

In these years, ablution never came. I still think of
your sheets on a bed, in an old hotel room where Oscar
Wilde once laid his head. Fortunes shared, debts made.
That night, with bottled up worship,
we uncorked an impossible horizon line.

Seasons later, I am left to wonder, would you sing my
name? Would you forgo distance, and reason, if only I
hopped on a plane? Would you undo me as you undid
me then?

Tell me you want me. Undress me, I'll address you the
same.

Some days are for roving, others for routine. I hope
you think of me when the lights are low and night is
dim. I've been writing love letters to Berlin.

Chromosome Story

we look for it to give us our bearings,
ground us in
life's continuity

the past accommodates –
timbre of voice,
a blot of colour
along the tailbone,
the body's long memory

riddles of the past
line a maw of genealogy

hours,
years,
and small worth
devoured tracing
the branches of family trees

nearly every human cell
biological mementos
of the family
who came before us

science,
our genetic code,
as if a trunk
in the attic

my parents,
with everything they know,
hiding in
their living cells

cutting to the truth of us
after a century
of speculation and denial

no one
takes a DNA test
in a vacuum

your secrets fold with
their secrets,
they learn them
as you do,
whether you want to or not

millions of nucleotides
in continuous motion,
tossed up, generation
after generation

carried forth
by warriors,
by the kidnapped
and curious,

the hungry, the indulgent,
the saintly, the scared,
the lovesick forebears of us all

Wintering

Yes — the wintertime
needed you
often a snowflake was waiting
for you to notice it

an ocean wind gusts
toward you out of a distant
unknowing, or as you put
on your boots, a hot breath
cloud whispered to your soles

all of this was a test

but did you fail?
weren't you always expecting
the worst conditions

as if every
storm was your end?

you will find your place
in the season of things

Because We're Going to Camp Mockingee

in the truck, on the way up,
we talk around the meaning of marriage,
we find an uncharted knowing
driving down dirt roads, passing sheep,
old barns, soon-to-be-made memories, alpacas

by the time we make it to the highway,
we conclude, love is truce,
a pact to honour and protect
one another's solitudes

wedding guests come from faraway places —
Iceland, Montréal, Calgary, Toronto —
to witness your wilderness love
many note: romance can be found in
late night coffee shop Hawaiian donuts

your love holds space for tenderness,
tent city, bar, Camp Mockingee
and most boldly: Just Married

your love is tied up in vintage floral bowties,
a bear and fox, dancing together
to 90s hits, stealing glances across summer camp

your love is a Rae Spoon song,
"Habitation" read aloud,
"Short Talk on the Sensation of Airplane Takeoff,"
"Ocean" as both guest and poem

your love is Atlantic,
resilient and resounding,
a place to live by,
an essential to life's raft

your love never forgets to bring
the condiments, it sports matching plaid,
it leans in, and looks out

your love is handsome new haircuts,
first canoe paddles, spines along dock,
eyes up to the Milky Way
a savoured last bite of campfire s'more

while you carve out a space to spend
the rest of your days together,
watching re-runs of *Roseanne*,
remembering all this

In Views of Keji

we find our muscles sore after a long canoe in
recuperate on a private island with a beach,
where a tree bends, grown horizontal towards land,
instead of sky

we swim, our bodies restored by
protected warm lake waters

at night, we sleep under a marquee of stars,
trees sway in the wind, loons call out late into the
hours,
a waning stag moon keeps a close eye

we weather the weather
lightning storms, rumbles of thunder
with bourbon and wine in our bellies

may we always see one another off
into the night
some from shoreline, others by canoe
and trust moonlight to lead the way

come morning, may we meet again
for lavender, lemon zest flapjacks,
Irish coffee, and bacon-laced on sticks
cooked over campfire

A School of Nightswimmers

It's the naked
who made this place and held it
in the roar of an era when
we reached outside of ourselves,
naively, goofy, dancing —
naked, naked, beautifully naked.
— BRIAN BRETT, "The Wreck"

in Pacific waters,
phosphorescence shimmers
we squint into thin light,
only mountain shadows visible
from our backs, floating outside
ourselves, beyond text, our insides
turned out, oceanbound

too late to call it night,
too early to be morning—
in-between time—we know
one another by breaks,
stanzas, splashes of water,
swim until our fingers prune

back ashore, wordy bodies shiver
recalling the mind's gravity
as we warm ourselves by fire,
huddled together in heaps
of exhaustion, intertwined

Paper Snowflakes and Sailboats

We slow danced to an old jazz standard
by low-burning tea lights.

I heard your Soviet watch tick in my ear,
the one you wind daily
to keep yourself in time.

I bleached the sheets
and made a headboard
of sails from your pillowcases.

I called your name
into a clawing night
and asked you to
uncork the champagne,
finish the blue cheese.

I left paper snowflakes
before midnight unwound
on your doorstep.

This, my deep swell
ocean lover
this, is our time.

This Renaissance

When I met you,
we spoke slowly,
memorized the pitch
and poise
of one another

you told me you held
a hundred sweet nothings
under your tongue

it was the sound of
my voice
and letters
that stirred you

your hands
twice the size
laced through my fingers
our palms held
down the tablecloth

you confessed
each day you lose
more of your sight
every hour
grows opaque
there are no streams of light

you'll go blind
in a few years
lose your ability to work

you say no one
wants a visual artist
deafened to life

I cupped my hands
over your eyes
and whispered:
there is a symphony
awaiting you

Our Tribe

We travel in time
light and space
in search of another

we find ourselves in constellations
old kitchens
the ocean floor

we meet at the mouth of the kingdom
near the seawall
wait for dusk

we yearn for the season to end
to come undone
wonder if we're wrong

we blend and blur
until the hour arrives
when we could give name
to ourselves
recall our collection of self
prove our kin

Wilderness Ceremony

lake bathing, sun worshipping,
tarp hanging
ceremonies of wilderness

you call out to the wild
it calls back

when wind picks up
waves roll over

you show me a black and gold spotted beetle,
I question your intention
lady bugs are known to bring good luck

here we are, late nights fireside,
long afternoon naps

nature's patterns remind us of a cycle
we are only small brass instruments
in the woodland orchestra

Amelia Blue (The Miraculous One)

In Havana's city of the dead
a grave of La Milagrosa,
Spanish for Miraculous One,
Amelia Goyri de Adot
who died in childbirth at the turn of the century

her infant son buried
in her coffin,
a child laid to rest at her feet

visitors flock to the cemetery outside
Plaza of the Revolution
her husband, Eduardo, visited three times a day,
grief-sick, left flowers,
knocked with three brass rings on her grave,
wanted her to know he came

walking backwards as he left,
he always hoped she could see him
looking out for signs of her
years pass until Amelia is exhumed,
her body discovered uncorrupted
Roman Catholics call this a sign of sanctity,
her nameless baby now cradled in her arms

a woman of miracles,
story spread, thousands of pilgrims gather at her grave,
leave their troubles at her feet, repeat Eduardo's rituals,
offer up prayer and touch the hem of her skirt

she becomes a beacon,
a translator between mankind and God

Last View of Bell Island

the funeral procession led
our family up a steep cliff,
an island cradled by an island,
to stand tall together
in an overgrown graveyard

a box of ashes in the back of the
priest's trunk
a day where the royal blue ocean
met a cloudless September sky
our foreheads and noses all sunburnt

even the whales greeted
the boat on her farewell journey
between Portugal Cove and Bell Island

only those oceanic jellyfish,
sea creatures, and seals
could recall her maiden voyage
78 years ago. The belle of the bay
left rolling hills, weathered
rocks, her family, and set
sights on the mainland

back in those days of plentiful
fish, youthful undoing,
high winds, and deep swells,
before loss became constant

we listen to the black-cloaked priest
sing a death hymn,
only grandfather hummed along,
like an out-of-tune baritone

the same voice sang out the night
she died, an old love song
to help ease her transition

to think they could doubt my love
yet today my love has flown away
I am without my love

at the grave, the minister placed
our letters into a velvet sack

daughters' and grandchildren's
blue eyes glistened like the water

she returned to the dirt,
where her mother's tomb,
a square big enough for a wooden box of ash,
and gravestone reminds us
she died on the same day
as her mother's birth

we dropped our tears, rocks,
a cigarette into the grave,
held one another close,
my grandfather murmured—

tears I cannot hide
oh, so I smile and say
when a lovely flame dies
smoke gets in your eyes

Fire on Lake Echo

on the last day of June
at a summer party, after sunset
two fire starters glide onto water
stand tall on paddleboards
to mirror fading light
on a lake that echoes

they set their gloved hands ablaze
become flame throwers
twin fireflies burn a mirage of
wild reflections on water

onlookers, partygoers, observers
drinks in hand, buzzed in conversation
hush to lean in close, listen to flames

these baton-whirlers, swirl and twirl
toss inferno over water
and nearly set
the lake on fire

Seeing Double

Remember when we sailed the world two by two? This is what I forgot to tell you.

The past wants me to tell you all it didn't want. Instead of remembering, we should just stay where we are and tend to things best we can. It wants me to say it earns a living by never returning and it's not about to now. It's thankful for the memory and snapshots but, really, it likes being something out of range. It's out of reach, so stop searching, stop seeking. It has a whole historiography of things that did or didn't happen, it can't take all the blame for the present. All of this, ours. Reflect and after time, let it go. Hold a ceremony, a burial, a wake. Grieve. Breathe. Deeper. Repeat. Grieve again. Stay up as late as you can to realize every hour follows another. Say a prayer for the thing you've done, say another for what you didn't say. Save your last prayer for what could have been but will never be. The past is a machine breaking down, loose screws and overstrained joints. You will come in first and last in this marathon. Our place is now, our cross-step.

Other Waves of Thought

these spirits of place
are ancient

you remember landscapes
landscapes
remember you

every view holds memory
all horizons meet the horizon within

quiet mind
quiet body
there is nothing more to this

from this shore to that
avoid rocks, bottom,
high winds and water
it calls lightning to its breast

these rituals
meditations of undoing
all of us breath

Tell Me, Medicine Woman, Who Do I Belong To?

once I was a fatherless daughter
now I come from a landless band
from west coast newfound land
where earth meets coast

I am an Irish-named river
born close to a mountain
married to the ocean
uncertain of my sense of place
now father's last name echoes
on the wind

I am Qalipu Mi'kmaq
product of the Indian Act
he's a man of few words
has never built a teepee
shingles suburban houses
only ladder touches ground

I try to sing to you
in Gaelic, English,
French and Mi'kmaw
but don't know your languages

you were hunter, trapper
healer, and bootlegger
a midwife to seven hundred babies
around Bay of St. Georges

you travelled by dog team
horse, sled, and snowshoes
to expectant mothers
father says you were small,
only four feet tall

you bring gifts –
eagle feathers, rock, tree bark –
to remind me of a place
in the possibilities,
woman, you are mighty